CHRISTIAN IV

"Her skal byen ligge!"

"Here the town shall lie!"

"Hier soll die Stadt liegen!"

"La ville se situera ici!"

"Aquí se erguirá la Ciudad!"

OSLO

Printed 1993 by KINA Italia SpA
Text: Jac. Brun. Layout: Dino Sassi
ISBN 82-7182-055-9 hf.
ISBN 82-7182-056-7 ib.
© NORMANNS KUNSTFORLAG A/S, OSLO

Normann
NORMANNS KUNSTFORLAG A/S, OSLO

Oslo vokste frem som et lite handelssted omkring år 1048 innerst i Oslofjorden, men allerede i jernalderen var det markedsplass her med buer, hus og naust. En rekke branner herjet hovedstaden under Ekeberg, og etter brannen i 1624 besluttet Christian IV at byen skulle flyttes til den andre siden av Akerselven, til området rundt Akershus festning, og den nye byen fristet en skiftende tilværelse med kriger, branner og farsotter, men også med fremgang og vekst. Byen fikk universitet i 1811, og etter at Norge fikk sin selvstendighet i 1814, ble Christiania det naturlige sentrum for landets administrasjon. I 1925 tok byen igjen navnet Oslo. I dag er Oslo en by med ca. 450.000 innbyggere, den fyller hele området rundt indre Oslofjord, og er berømt for sin vakre beliggenhet og sine storslagne omgivelser.
Foruten Det kongelige slott og Stortinget, som begge ligger ved byens hovedgate "Karl Johan", har byen en rekke severdigheter. Kunstmaleren Edvard Munch skjenket alle sine arbeider til Oslo Kommune, og de er nå samlet i et eget museum som bærer hans navn.
Kon-Tiki flåten som Thor Heyerdahl benyttet på sin ferd over Stillehavet i 1947, har fått sitt eget museum på Bygdøy. Ikke langt dørfra finner vi polarskipet "Fram", vikingskipene som ble bygget i det 9. århundre e.K. og Norsk Folkemuseum med bygninger og folkekunst fra hele landet.
Vigelands skulpturpark er også en av byens store severdigheter og likeledes Holmenkollbakken litt utenfor selve bykjernen.

The Oslo of today has evolved from a modest trading centre, founded round about 1048 at the head of the fjord of the same name, but as far back as the Iron Age there was a marketplace on the site, surrounded by a huddle of rude huts, boathouses, and other buildings. Time and again, however, the capital beneath the heights of Ekeberg was ravaged by fire, and after a last big blaze in 1624 King Christian IV resolved that it should be rebuilt on the other side of the Aker river, close to Akershus Castle. Renamed Christiania, the new town continued to prosper and expand, despite a series of setbacks that included war, fire, and pestilence. In 1811 it was honoured with a university of its own, and after dissolution of the union with Denmark in 1814 it automatically assumed the role of national administrative centre. In 1925 the town readopted its original name of Oslo. Present-day Oslo has a population of 450,000. Occupying the whole of the area around the inner reaches of the fjord, it is a modern city noted for its scenic location and superb natural surroundings.
The Royal Palace and the parliament building (Storting) are but two of Oslo's many attractions. The painter Edvard Munch bequeathed the bulk of his work to the city, which erected a special building, the Munch Museum, to house them.
The Kon-Tiki raft, on which Thor Heyerdahl crossed the Pacific in 1947, likewise occupies a museum of its own. Standing on the Bygdøy peninsula, just across the harbour, it is only a stone's throw from other notable relics of the past – the polar exploration vessel "Fram", two ninth-century Viking ships, and the Norwegian Folk Museum, a comprehensive collection of rustic buildings and folk art drawn from all over Norway.
Other major attractions include the Vigeland Sculpture Park and, in the hills above the city, the Holmenkollen Ski Jump.

Oslo wuchs um das Jahr 1048 am innersten Oslofjord als eine kleine Handelsstadt heran, aber bereits in der Eisenzeit war hier Jahrmarktsplatz mit Buden, Häusern und Kahnschuppen. Eine Reihe von Bränden verwüsteten die unterhalb des Ekeberg gelegene Hauptstadt, und nach der Feuersbrunst 1624 fasste Christian IV. den Entschluss, dass die Stadt nach der anderen Seite des Flusses Akerselven verlegt werden sollte, hin zum Gebiet um die Festung Akershus, und die neue Stadt erhielt den Namen Christiania. Jahrhunderte hindurch hat die Stadt ein wechselndes Dasein geführt mit Kriegen, Bränden und Epidemien, aber auch mit Fortschritten und Wachstum. Die Universität erhielt die Stadt 1811, und nachdem Norwegen im Jahre 1814 seine Selbständigkeit erhalten hat, wurde Christiania das natürliche Zentrum für die Verwaltung des Landes. Im Jahre 1925 nahm die Stadt ihren ursprünglichen Namen Oslo wieder an. Heute ist Oslo eine Stadt von ca. 450.000 Einwohnern, sie umfasst das gesamte Gebiet um den inneren Oslofjord und ist wegen ihrer hübschen Lage und der grossartigen Umgebung berühmt. Ausser dem königlichen Schloss und dem Storting (Reichstag), beide an der Hauptstrasse "Karl Johan" gelegen, hat die Stadt eine Reihe von Sehenswürdigkeiten. Der Kunstmaler Edvard Munch vermachte alle seine Arbeiten der Stadt Oslo, und jetzt befinden sie sich in einem besonderen Museum, das seinen Namen trägt. Das Kon-Tiki-Floss, das Thor Heyerdahl auf seiner Fahrt über den Stillen Ozean im Jahre 1947 benutzte, hat sein eigenes Museum auf der Halbinsel Bygdøy. Nicht weit vom Floss entfernt findet man das Polarschiff "Fram", die Wikingerschiffe, gebaut im 9. Jahrhundert n.Chr., und das Norwegische Volkmuseum mit Gebäuden und Volkskunst vom ganzen Land. Vigelands Skulpturenpark ist auch eine der grossen Sehenswürdigkeiten der Stadt, ebenso die Holmenkollenschanze etwas ausserhalb des eigentlichen Stadtkerns.

Oslo, située au fin fond du fjord du même nom, devint une petite place commerciale en 1048. Or, dès l'âge de fer un marché composé de voûtes, de maisons et de hangars existait déjà à cet emplacement. Plusieurs incendies ravagèrent la capitale en aval de la colline d'Ekeberg. Ainsi, à la suite de l'incendie de 1624, le roi Christian IV décida de transposer la ville autour du chateau-fort d'Akershus de l'autre côté du fleuve d'Aker. Cette nouvelle ville qui se construisit fut baptisée Christiania. Christiania, bien que ravagée par des guerres, des incendies et des épidémies, connut une certaine prospérité et croissance. L'Université fut construite en 1811, et après que la Norvège eut obtenu son indépendance en 1814, Christiania devint le centre naturel pour l'administration du pays. En 1925 la ville fut rebaptisée Oslo. Aujourd'hui, Oslo compte 450.000 habitants et s'étend le long du fjord d'Oslo. Oslo est renommée pour son merveilleux site et ses environs naturels grandioses.
Outre le Palais Royal et le Parlement qui tous deux se trouvent sur l'artère principale de Karl Johan, Oslo comporte de nombreux sites culturels. Le musée Edvard Munch abrite toutes les œuvres du célèbre peintre norvégien Edvard Munch offertes par celui-ci à la municipalité d'Oslo.
Le radeau Kon-Tiki que Thor Heyerdahl utilisa pour traverser le Pacifique en 1947 est exposé au musée Kon-Tiki dans la péninsule de Bygdø. Deux autres musées, près du Kon-Tiki, abritent le navire polaire "Fram" et le musée des drakkars construits par les Viking au 9e siècle. Des villages reconstitués au musée populaire norvégien également situé à Bygdøy, donnet un aperçu des constructions anciennes en bois et des objets d'art populaire au cours des siècles. Au centre de la ville, le parc Vigeland a été créé pour recevoir les sculptures de ce grand artiste national. Sur les hauteurs de la ville, se trouve le célèbre tremplin de ski d'Holmenkollen.

Oslo emergió como un pequeño centro comercial hacia el año 1048 en las entrañas del fiordo de Oslo, pero ya en la edad de hierro existía aquí feria con arcadas, casas y cobertizos. Un sinnúmero de incendios devastó la ciudad bajo Ekeberg, y después del incendio de 1624 Christian el IV decidió que la ciudad sea levantada de nuevo en el otro lado del Rìo de Aker, en la zona de los alrededores del Castillo de Akershus y a esta nueva ciudad se le dió el nombre de Christiania. A través de los centenarios la ciudad ha pasado distintas épocas de guerras, incendios y epidemias, pero también con progreso y crecimiento. Se fundó su Universidad en 1811, y después de lograr su independencia en 1814, Christiania se transformó en centro natural de la administración del país. En 1925 la Ciudad volvió a llamarse Oslo. Hoy Oslo es una ciudad de unos 450.000 habitantes, ocupa toda la zona alrededor del interior del fiordo de Oslo y es conocida por su preciosa localidad y sus impresionantes alrededores.
Además del Palacio Real y el Parlamento, que ambos se encuentran en la calle principal "Karl Johan", la Ciudad tiene unas cuantas cosas que deben ser vistas. El pintor Edvard Munch obsequió todas sus obras a la Municipalidad de Oslo y están reunidas en un Museo que lleva su nombre.
La balsa Kon-Tiki, utilizada por Thor Heyerdahl eb su travesía del Pacífico en 1947, tiene su propio Museo en Bygdøy. Y no lejos de ésta se encuentra el buque polar "Fram", los barcos vikingos que fueron construidos en el 9º centenario d.C. y el Museo Nacional con edificios y artesanía de todo el país.
El parque de esculturas de Vigeland es también una de las atracciones así como los Saltos de Holmenkollen en las afueras de la Ciudad.

Sjømennenes minnesmerke på
Bygdøy. Oslo har alltid vært en
sjøfartsby, og den har landets
travleste havn. Passasjer- og
lasteskip forbinder Oslo med
alle landene rundt Nordsjøen.

The Seamen's Memorial,
Bygdøy. Oslo has always been
a thriving seaport, and its
harbour is the busiest in the
country. Passenger ships and
freighters link the capital with
all the countries bordering on
the North Sea.

Das Denkmal der Seeleute auf Bygdöy. Oslo ist stets eine Seefahrtsstadt gewesen, und sie hat den lebhaftesten Hafen des Landes. Passagier- und Frachtschiffe verbinden Oslo mit allen Ländern an der Nordsee.

Le monument commémoratif des marins à Bygdøy. Oslo, ville maritime depuis toujours, a le plus grand port du pays. Les paquebots et les cargos relient Oslo à tous les pays de la Mer du Nord.

Memorial a los marineros en Bygdøy. Oslo ha sido siempre una ciudad marinera, y tiene el puerto más activo del país. Buques de pasajeros y de carga enlazan a Oslo con todos los paises Mar del Norte.

▲ BOUND FOR OSLO   ▼CHRISTIAN RADICH

Akershus, festningen som aldri er blitt beseiret,
ble bygget av Håkon Magnusson ca. 1300.

Besieged but never conquered, Akershus
Castle was built in about 1300 by King Håkon V
Magnusson.

Die Festung Akershus, die nie besiegt worden
ist, wurde ca. 1300 von Håkon Magnusson
gebaut.

Akershus – la forteresse imprenable – fut bâtie
vers l'an 1300 par Håkon Magnusson.

Akershus, la fortaleza que nunca ha sido
tomada, fué construida por Haakon Magnusson
hacia el año 1300.

Akershus slott ligger som et verdig minnesmerke fra vår fortid, om natten som en flombelyst juvel. I våre dager er slottet restaurert og ført tilbake til sitt gamle utseende, og det benyttes som representasjonslokaler for regjeringen.

A proud historical monument, at night Akershus Castle is bathed in floodlights. The castle has been painstakingly restored and many important government functions are held in its spacious halls.

Das Schloss Akershus bildet ein würdiges Denkmal unserer Vergangenheit und wirkt nachts wie ein flutbeleuchtetes Juwel. Jetzt ist das Schloss restauriert, hat wieder sein altes Aussehen bekommen, und es wird bei besonderen Anlössen von der Regierung für Repräsentationszwecke benutzt.

Le château d'Akershus – digne vestige de notre passé – resplendit comme un véritable joyau sous les projecteurs. Restauré et rendu à sa beauté primitive, le château sert aujourd'hui de locaux de représentation officielle.

El Castillo de Akershus se alza, como valioso tetamento de nuestro pasado, por la noche como una joya iluminada. Actualmente el Castilla esta restaurado y ha vuelto a recobrar su apariencia original y es utilizado como locales de representación por el Gobierno.

Akershus slott. Øverst til venstre ser vi Olavshallen og til høyre Christian IV. sal. Til høyre ser vi det nasjonale krigsminnesmerke som ble reist etter siste verdenskrig.

Akershus Castle. Top left: King Olav Hall. Above: Christian IV Hall. Bottom right: The national memorial to the fallen of World War II.

Schloss Akershus. Ganz oben links sehen wir den Olavssaal und rechts den Saal Christian IV. Rechts ist das nationale Kriegsdenkmal, errichtet nach dem letzten Weltkrieg.

La château d'Akershus. En haut, à gauche, la Salle dite "Salle Olav" et à droite la Salle Christian IV. A droite le Monument National aux Morts de la dernière guerre.

El Castillo de Akershus, Más arriba, a la izquierda, vemos la Sala de Olav y, a la derecha, la Sala de Christian IV. A la derecha vemos el Monumento Nacional conmemorativo de la guerra que fué erigido despues de la última guerra mundial.

Oslo sentrum har idag et rikt varierende liv
og en sjarmerende blanding av ny og gammel
arkitektur.

Oslo's busy city centre, with its delightful blend
of buildings old and new.

Die Stadtmitte Oslos hat heute ein sehr reges
Leben und eine reizvolle Mischung neuer und
alter Architektur.

Le Centre d'Oslo présente aujourd'hui une vie
richement variée, dans un charmant mélange
d'architecture moderne et ancienne.

El Centro de Oslo tiene actualmente una rica
y variada vida y una atractiva mezcla de
arquitectura antigua y moderna.

Oslo Rådhus.

Oslo Town Hall.

Das Osloer Rathaus.

L'Hotel de Ville.

Ayuntamiento de Oslo.

Oslo Rådhus ble påbegynt i 1931, og byggearbeidet skred raskt frem under ledelse av arkitektene Arnstein Arneberg og Magnus Paulsson frem til 1940 da den annen verdenskrig forsinket fullførelsen. Byggearbeidet fortsatte for fullt etter krigen, og de norske kunstnerne fikk store og krevende oppgaver med utsmykkinger både ute og inne. Den høytidelige åpning fant sted 15. mai 1950.

The foundation stone of Oslo's Town Hall was laid in 1931. Under the supervision of two noted architects building proceeded apace, until the war intervened. With the coming of peace work was resumed, and Norwegian artists and sculptors applied themselves to the challenging task of embellishing the new building, inside and out. The official opening took place on 15 May 1950.

Der Bau des Osloer Rathauses wurde 1931 begonnen, die Bauarbeiten schritten schnell voran unter Leitung der Architekten Arnstein Arneberg und Magnus Paulsson bis 1940 als der zweite Weltkrieg die Fertigstellung verzögerte. Nach dem Kriege setzten die Bauarbeiten eifrig fort, und die norwegischen Künstler erhielten grosse Anforderungen stellende Aufgaben mit externen und internen Ausschmükkungen. Die feierliche Einweihung erfolgte am 15. Mai 1950.

Commencé en 1931, l'Hotel de Ville s'éleva rapidement sous la conduite des architectes Arnstein Arneberg et Magnus Poulsson, jusqu'à ce que la Seconde Guerre Mondiale – en 1940 – vînt en interrompre l'achèvement. Les travaux reprirent à plein après la guerre, et les artistes norvégiens se trouvèrent confrontés à d'immenses tâches décoratives, tant à l'extérieur qu'à l'intérieur. L'inauguration solennelle eut lieu le 15 Mai 1950.

El Ayuntamiento de Oslo fué empezado en 1931, y los trabajos fueron llevados a cabo efectivamente bajo la direccción de los arquitectos Arnstein Arneberg y Magnus Paulsson hasta 1940, ya que la segunda guerra mundial impidió su terminación. Los trabajos de construcción fueron reanudados rápidamente despues de la guerra y se encargó a artistas noruegos que se ocuparan de grandes y exigentes obras de decoración internas y externas. La ceremonia solemne de inauguración tuvo lugar el 15 de mayo de 1950.

Sentralhallen i Rådhuset med Alf Rolfsens fresko-maleri øverst og Henrik Sørensens oljemaleri nederst. Til høyre svanene i Borggården utført av Dyre Vaa.

Oslo Town Hall. Two views of the Central Hall embracing (left) a fresco by Alf Rolfsen and (below) an oil painting by Henrik Sørensen. Right: Dyre Vaa's gilded swans in the forecourt.

Die grosse Rathaushalle mit Alf Rolfsens Fresko-gemälde ganz oben und Henrik Sörensens Ölge-mälde ganz unten. Rechts die Schwäne im Burghof, ausgeführt von Dyre Vaa.

Le grand hall central. En haut, la fresque d'Alf Rolfsen. En bas l'immense toile de Henrik Sørensen. A droite les Cygnes de la Cour d'Honneur, sculpture de Dyre Vaa.

La Sala Central del Municipio con pinturas al fresco de Alf Rolfsen, más arriba, el óleo de Henrik Sørensen, más abajo. A la derecha, los Cisnes en el Patio, por Dyre Vaa.

Festgalleriet (over) er dekorert av Axel Revold og utstyrt med tepper som er vevet av Kåre Mikkelsen Jonsborg. Til venstre skulptur av Emil Lie.

The Festival Gallery (above) was decorated by Axel Revold and the walls are hung with tapestries woven by Kåre Mikkelsen Jonsborg. Left: A statue by Emil Lie.

Die Festgalerie (darüber) ist von Axel Revold dekoriert und mit Teppichen ausgestattet, die Kåre Mikkelsen Jonsborg gewebt hat. Links die Skulptur von Emil Lie.

Au-dessus du Hall, la Galerie des Fêtes, décorée par Axel Revold et garnie de tapis tissés par Kåre Mikkelsen Jonsborg. A Gauche, une oeuvre du sculpteur Emil Lie.

La Galería de Fiestas (arriba) esta decorada por Axel Revold y esta equipada con tapices tejidos por Kåre Mikkelsen Jonsborg. A la izquierda escultura de Emil Lie.

Nasjonalteatret
The National Theatre
Das Nationaltheater
Le Théâtre National
El Theatro Nacional

Vika i gamle dager et strøk som var preget av fattigdom
og forfall. Idag er strøket preget av moderne forretnings-
og kontorbygg. Her finner man også Oslo nye konserthus.

Once an area marked by poverty and tumbledown houses,
Vika is now dominated by modern shops and office blocks.
The area also encompasses Oslo's new concert hall.

Vika war ehedem eine Gegend, die von Armut und Verfall
war. Das heutige Gepräge sind moderne Geschäfts-
und Bürohäuser. Hier findet man auch Oslos neue Konzerthaus.

Vika était autrefois un quartier pauvre et délabré.
Aujourd'hui on y trouve de beaux magasins modernes et
de confortables immeubles de bureaux. La nouvelle salle
de concert d'Oslo.

Antaño era Vika un barrio que se distinguía por su pobreza
y decadencia. Hoy la zona se destaca por sus modernos edificios
de comercio y oficinas. Aquí encontramos también la nueva
Casa de Conciertos de Oslo.

Feiring av nasjonaldagen 17. mai foran slottet

A Constitution Day (17 May) parade in front of the
Royal Palace

17 Mai vor dem Königlichen Schloss

Le jour de la fête nationale (17 mai) devant le Palais
royal

La fiesta Nacional (17 mai) ante el Palacio Real

Oslo har et rikt utvalg av skulpturer. Nedenfor ser vi Gustav Vigelands monument over matematikeren Niels Henrik Abel. Til høyre dronning Maud hugget i granitt av Ada Madssen.

Oslo is richly endowed with statues, among them Gustav Vigeland's monument to the mathematician Niels Henrik Abel (below) and (right) a granite statue of Queen Maud by Ada Madssen.

Oslo hat eine reiche Auswahl von Skulpturen. Unten sehen wir Gustav Vigelands Monument über den Mathematiker Niels Henrik Abel. Rechts Königin Maud, ausgehauen aus Granit von Ada Madssen.

Oslo s'orne de multiples statues. Ci-dessous le monument de Gustav Vigeland à la mémoire du Mathématicien Niels Henrik Abel. A droite. la Reine Maud, sculptée dans le granit par Ada Madssen.

Oslo tiene un rico surtido de estatuas. Abajo vemos el monumento hecho por Gustav Vigeland del matemático Niels Henrik Abel. A la derecha la Reina Maud hecha en granito por Ada Madssen.

AKER BRYGGE

▲ AKER BRYGGE   ▼DAM STREDET

Midt i byens travle for-
retningstrøk finner vi
intime restauranter som
har uteservering i den
varme årstiden.

Downtown Oslo boasts
an abundance of intimate
restaurants, many of
which offer outdoor
service in the summer.

Mitten in der lebhaften
Geschäftsgegend der
Stadt gibt es intime
Restaurants, wo in der
warmen Jahreszeit auch
draussen serviert wird.

Au centre ville, de petits
restaurants intimes
servent en été sur leurs
terrasses plein-air.

En medio de las activa
calles centrales
encontramos también
íntimos restaurantes.

Byens gamle Universitet

The old University

Die alte Universität der Stadt

(En haut) L'ancienne Université d'Oslo

La vieja Universidad de la Ciudad

Like ved Karl Johansgate, Oslos hovedgate, finner vi
Studenterlunden med sine sprudlende fontener.

Adjoining the busy main thoroughfare, Karl Johans gate, is
Studenterlunden, its plashing fountains flanked by avenues
of trees.

Dicht bei der Karl Johans gate, der Hauptstrasse Oslos,
befindet sich Studenterlunden, ein Park mit sprudelnden
Fontänen.

Tout près de l'avenue Karl Johan, l'artère principale d'Oslo,
le "Bosquet des Etudiants" avec ses rafraîchissantes fontaines

Cerca de la Calle Carl Johan, la principal de Oslo, encontram
el Studenterlunden con sus fuentes.

Stortorget er byens blomstermarked, og her finner vi
Christian IV., den moderne bys grunnlegger, som peker
ut hvor byen skal ligge.

Stortorget, Oslo's flower market, is overlooked by
a statue of King Christian IV, founder of the city,
pointing to his chosen site.

Stortorget ist der Blumenmarkt der Stadt, und hier steht
das Denkmal Christian IV., des Gründers der modernen
Stadt, welcher andeutet, wo die Stadt liegen soll.

Sur la Place du Grand Marché, le Marché aux Fleurs.
Christian IV, fondateur de la ville moderne, s'y dresse
sur son socle et désigne du doigt l'emplacement choisi.

La plaza principal Stortorget es el mercado de flores de
la ciudad y aquí encontramos a Christian IV, fundador
de la nueva ciudad, que esta señalando donde debe ser
construida la mesena.

Oslo Domkirke ble innviet i 1697, og mens eksteriøret forble uforandret gjennom det 18. århundre fikk interiøret en stadig rikere utsmykning. I 1850 fikk kirken sitt høyreiste, slanke tårn. og ved den siste restaureringen (fullført i 1950) fikk interiørene sitt nåværende utseende med takmalerier som er laget av Hugo Lous Mohr.

Oslo Cathedral was consecrated in 1697. While its exterior remained unchanged right up to the close of the 18th century, the interior underwent constant improvement and embellishment. The spire was added in 1850. Restoration of the interior to give it its present appearance was completed in 1960 and included the addition of ceiling murals by Hugo Lous Mohr.

Der Osloer Dom wurde 1697 eingeweiht, und während das Exterieur das 18. Jahrhundert hindurch unverändert blieb, erhielt das Interieur eine ständig reichere Ausschmückung. 1850 erhielt der Dom seinen hochragenden, schlanken Turm, und bei der letzten Restaurierung (vollendet 1950) bekamen die Interieurs ihr jetziges Aussehen mit Dekkengemälden, ausgeführt von Hugo Lous Mohr.

La Cathédrale d'Oslo, consacrée en 1697. L'extérieur ne subit aucun changement tout au long du XVIIIe siècle. L'intérieur, au contraire, s'enrichit constamment de nouvelles décorations. En 1850 s'éleva le clocher élancé, et lors des dernières restaurations (achevées en 1950) l'intérieur acquit son visage actuel, avec les fresques du plafond exécutées par Hugo Lous Mohr.

La Catedral de Oslo fué inaugurada en 1697 y mientras que el exterior peraneció sin cambios a través del siglo 18, su interior fué adquiriendo una decoración cada vez más rica. En 1850 se construyó su esbelta torre y bajo su última restauración (culminada en 1950) se dió al interior su actual aspecto, con pinturas en el techo hechas por Hugo Lous Mohr.

Stortinget er Norges nasjonalforsamling.
Her sitter 165 representanter som velges
ved stortingsvalg hvert 4 år

The Storting, Norway's national assembly
comprises 165 members. Elections are
held every four years

Das Storting ist Norwegens National
versammlung. Hier sitzen 165.
Abgeordnete, die alle 4 Jahre bei den
Stortingswahlen gewähtl werden

Le Storting est l'Assemblée Nationale
norvégienne. 165 représentants y siègent,
èlus, tous les 4 ans

El Storting es la Asemblea Nacional Aqui
trabajan 165 representantes que son
elegidos por elecciones parlamentarias
cada cuatro anos

Gustav Vigelands (1869–1943) skulpturpark er verdens største samling av
skulpturer utført av én person. På 320
mål har han plassert 192 skulpturer med
tilsammen 650 figurer. Her har han
skildret menneskenes vandring på
jorden fra mors liv til graven.

The sculpture park that bears his name is
the world's largest collection of sculptures executed by one single artist –
Gustav Vigeland (1869–1943). Eighty
acres (3¼ sq. km) in area, the park
encompasses no less than 192 pieces of
statuary – 650 figures – illustrating man's
journey from womb to tomb.

Gustav Vigelands (1869–1943) Skulpturenpark ist die grösste nur von einer
Person ausgeführte Skulpturensammlung
der Welt. Auf 320 Dekar hat er 192
Skulpturen mit insgesamt 650 Figuren
placiert. Hier hat er die Wanderung der
Menschen auf der Erde vom Mutterleib
bis zum Grabe geschildert.

Le parc de Gustav Vigeland (1869–1943)
rassemble la plus grande collection
existant dans le monde, de sculptures
exécutées par un seul homme. 192
groupes sculptés, totalisant 650 figures,
réunis sur 320 ares. Le cheminement de
l'homme sur terre y est décrit, depuis le
sein maternel jusqu'à la tombe.

El Parque de Esculturas de Gustav
Vigeland (1862–1943) tiene la colección
de esculturas hechas por una persona
mayor del mundo. 192 esculturas
emplazadas en 320.000 m², con un total
de 650 figuras. Aqui ha expresado el
sendero humano en esta tierra, desde el
vientre de su madre hasta su tumba.

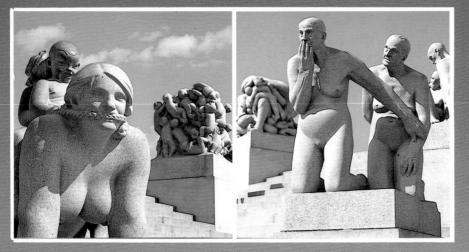

Monolitten.

The Monolith.

Der Monolith.

Le Monolithe.

El monolito.

Detaljer fra Vigelands skulpturpark.

Details from the Vigeland Sculpture Park.

Details von Vigelands Skulpturenpark.

Le Parc de Vigeland. Détails.

Detalles del Parque de Esulturas de Vigeland.

Til venstre ser vi 4 skulpturer fra broen i Vigelandsparken. Ovenfor ser vi et parti fra Vigelandsmuseet som ligger like ved Vigelandsparken. Huset ble bygget som atelier og bolig for Gustav Vigeland av Oslo kommune, til gjengjeld ga Vigeland nesten hele sin produksjon til byen. En enestående kontrakt var dermed inngått mellom en by og en kunstner. I 1924 flyttet Vigeland inn i det nye, store bygg. I 1947 åpnet museet, som rommer ca. 1600 skulpturer. 12 000 tegninger og 420 tresnitt.

Left: Four statues surmounting the bridge in the Vigeland Sculpture Park. Above: A part of the Vigeland Museum adjoining the park. The municipal authorities erected this building as a studio and home for Gustav Vigeland, and in return the sculptor donated virtually all his works to the capital, a transaction between a city and an artist that was unique. Vigeland moved in in 1924, the building being opened as a museum in 1947. It houses some 1600 sculptures, 12,000 drawings, and 420 woodcuts

Links sehen wir 4 Skulpturen von der Brücke im Vigelandpark. Oben sehen wir eine Partie vom Vigelandmuseum, das dicht beim Vigelandpark liegt. Das Haus wurde von der Stadt Oslo als Atelier und Wohnung für Gustav Vigeland gebaut; dafür gab Viegland der Stadt fast seine ganze Produktion. Ein einzigartiger Vertrag war damit zwischen einer Stadt und einem Künstler geschlossen. 1924 zog Vigeland in das neue, grosse Haus ein. 1947 wurde das Museum eröffnet, das ca. 1600 Skulpturen, 12.000 Zeichnungen und 420 Holzschnitte birgt.

A gauche, 4 sculptures ornant le pont du Parc Vigeland. Au-dessus on aperçoit le Musée Vigeland, tout près du Parc. Le bâtiment fut construit par la Municipalité, pour servir à Gustav Vigeland d'atelier et de demeure. En revanche, Vigeland fit don à la Ville de la presque totalité de son oeuvre. C'était là un contrat unique en son genre passé entre une ville et un artiste. En 1924 Vigeland prit possession de la place. En 1947 s'ouvrit le Musée: 1600 sculptures, 12000 dessins et 420 gravures sur bois.

A la izquierda vemos cuatro esculturas del puente en el Parque de Vigeland. Arriba vemos una parte del Museo de Vigeland que cerca del Parque de Vigeland. La casa fié construida como taller y residencia para Gustav Vigeland por el Ayuntamiento de Oslo, a cambio Vigeland donó casi toda su producción a la ciudad. Un contrato excepcional fué contraido una ciudad y un artista. En 1924 se mudó Vigeland al nuevo y grande edificio. En 1947 se abrió el Museo, que contiene 1600 esculturas, 12.000 dibujos y 420 tallados de madera.

Nedenfor ser vi "Akademikeren", til høyre Osebergskipet
og Gokstadskipet.
© Copyright: Universitetets Oldsaksamling.

Below: A carved headpost from the Oseberg ship. Right: The
Oseberg and Gokstad ships, relics of the Viking Age.
© Copyright: Oslo University Collection of Antiquities.

Unten sehen wir "Akademikeren", rechts das Osebergschiff
und das Gokstadschiff.
© Copyright: Altertumssammlung der Universität.

En bas, "l'Académicien"; à droite les vaisseaux vikings
d'Oseberg et de Gokstad.
© Copyright: La collection d'objets antiques de l'Université.

Abajo vemos el "Académico", a la derecha el buque de
Oseberg y el de Gokstad.

Til høyre: Gokstadskipet, bygget 850 e. Kr.
© Copyright: Universitetets Oldsaksamling.

Right: The Gokstad ship (850 AD).
© Copyright: Oslo University Collection of Antiquities.

Rechts: das Gokstadschiff, gebaut 850 n.Chr.
© Copyright: Altertumssammlung der Universität.

A droite: Le vaisseau de Gokstad, construit en l'an 850 (A.D.).
© Copyright: La collection d'objets antiques de l'Université.

Abajo vemos el "Académico", a la derecha el buque de Oseberg y el de Gokstad.

Vognen ovenfor og sleden til høyre er to av de rikt dekorerte gjenstandene som ble gravet ut sammen med Osebergskipet. Det var skikk bla vikingene å la de avdøde få med seg utstyr som de trengte for å fortsette sin gjerning i et liv etter døden.

The waggon above and the sledge on the right were both among the ornately decorated objects excavated with the Oseberg ship. The Vikings used to bury their dead with the accoutrements they were thought to need in the afterlife.

Der Wagen oben und der Schlitten rechts sind zwei der reich dekorierten Gegenstände, die zusammen mit dem Osebergschiff ausgegraben wurden. Unter den Wikingern war es Sitte, den Verstorbenen Ausstattung mitzugeben, die sie benötigten, um ihr un und Lassen in einem Leben nach dem Tode fortzusetzen.

Le chariot ci-dessus et le traîneau, à droite, richement décorés, font partie de l'inventaire extrait des fouilles où fut découvert le vaisseau d'Oseberg. Il était d'usage, chez les Vikings, d'enterrer les morts avec tout l'équipment nécessaire pour leur permettre de poursuivre leur oeuvre dans l'Au-delà.

El carro de arriba y el trineo a la derecha son dos de los objetos, ricamente decorados, que fueron descubiertos junto con el buque Oseberg. Era costumbre de los vikingos dejar que los muertos se llevaran el equipo que necesitaran para continuar su labor en otro vida despues de la muerte.

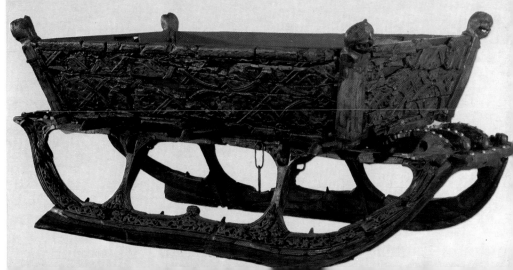

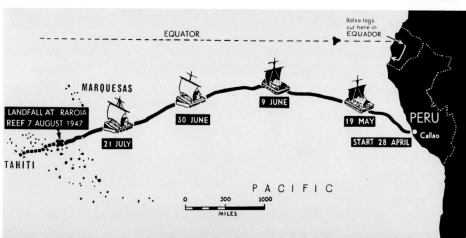

Balsa logs
cut here in
EQUATOR

EQUATOR

MARQUESAS

LANDFALL AT RAROIA
REEF 7 AUGUST 1947

30 JUNE

9 JUNE

19 MAY

PERU

Callao

21 JULY

START 28 APRIL

TAHITI

PACIFIC

0   500   1000

MILES

Balsaflåten Kon-Tiki har fått sitt eget museum på Bygdøy. Thor Heyerdahl sammen med 5 mann seilte 8000 km med den fra Peru til Raroia på Polynesia i løpet av 101 døgn fra 28. april til 7. august 1947.

Kon-Tiki, Thor Heyerdahl's balsa raft, is housed in a museum of its own on the Bygdøy Peninsula. In the space of 101 days (28 April – 7 August 1947) Heyerdahl and five companions sailed this raft 8000 kilometres, crossing from Peru to Raroia in Polynesia.

Das Balsafloss Kon-Tiki hat sein eigenes Museum auf der Halbinsel Bygdöy bekommen. Thor Heyerdahl segelte vom 28. April bis 7. August 1947 zusammen mit 5 Mann 8.000 km mit diesem Floss von Peru nach Raroia in Polynesien – 101 Tage und Nächte.

Le radeau de balsa, le Kon-Tiki, a son propre musée à Bygdøy. Le 28 Avril 1947, Thor Heyerdahl quittait le Pérou avec 5 compagnons, parcourait 8000 km. sur ce radeau et atteignait Raroia, en Polynésie, le 7 Août, après 101 jours de mer.

A la Balsa Kon-Tiki se le ha edificado su propio museo en Bygdøy. Thor Heyerdahl con cinco compañeros navegaron 8.000 km con esta balsa desde Perú a Raroia en Polinesia, viaje que duró 101 dias, desde el 28 abril al 7 agosto de 1947.

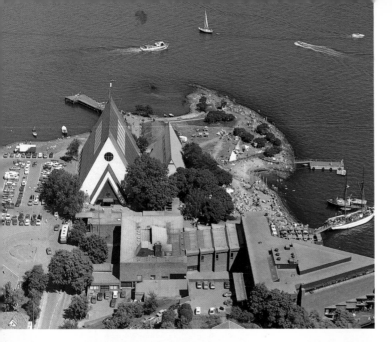

"Fram" ligger nå i trygg havn i sin egen bygning på Bygdøy. Skipet ble bygget for Fridtjof Nansen for at han skulle få fullføre sin drøm om å la seg drive med is og strøm over polhavet. På sin første ferd (1893–1896) drev "Fram" over polhavet som planlagt, men uten å nå selve polpunktet. På neste ferd (1898–1902) under Otto Sverdrups ledelse, ble den såkalte nordostpassasjen mellom Grønland og Canada utforsket, og på sin tredje ferd (1910–1914) seilte "Fram" under ledelse av Roald Amundsen helt ned til is-barrieren ved Sydpolen. Selv nådde han polpunktet den 14. desember 1911. Dermed er "Fram" det skip i verden som har vært lengst mot nord og lengst mot syd.

Snug from the elements in its own museum on the Bygdøy Peninsula, the "Fram" was originally built to enable Fridtjof Nansen to realise his dream of drifting with the pack and current clear across the Arctic Ocean. On its first attempt (1893–1896) the expedition completed the crossing but failed to reach the actual pole. On the vessel's second voyage (1898–1902) the Northeast Passage between Greenland and Canada was explored under the leadership of Otto Sverdrup. And on its third (1910–1914) Roald Amundsen sailed the "Fram" right down to the edge of the ice barring the way to the South Pole. He and four of his men reached the pole on 14 December 1911, the first to do so. These historic voyages mean that the "Fram" has sailed further north and further south than any other vessel in the world.

Die "Fram" liegt jetzt sicher untergebracht in einem eigenen Gebäude auf der Halbinsel Bygdöy. Das Schiff wurde für Fridtjof Nansen gebaut, damit er seinen Traum, sich durch Eis und Strömung übers Polarmeer treiben zu lassen, erfüllen konnte. Auf ihrer ersten Fahrt (1893–1896) trieb die "Fram" übers Polarmeer wie geplant, jedoch ohne den Polpunkt selbst erreicht zu haben. Auf ihrer nächsten Fahrt (1898–1902) unter Otto Sverdrups Leitung wurde die sogenannte Nordóstpassage zwischen Grönland und Kanada erforscht, und auf ihrer dritten Fahrt (1910–1914) fuhr die "Fram" unter der Leitung Roald Amundsens weit hinunter bis zur Eisbarriere in Südpol. Er selbst erreichte den Polpunkt am 14. Dezember 1911. Die "Fram" ist somit das Schiff in der Welt, das am weitesten gen Norden und am weitesten gen Süden fuhr.

Bien protégé par le bâtiment qui l'abrite, le "Fram" est définitivement ancré à Bygdøy. Le navire fut construit pour Fridtjof Nansen, afin de lui permettre de réaliser son rêve: se laisser dériver par les glaces et les courants de l'Océan arctique. La première expédition (1893–1896) réalisa cette dérive comme prévu; mais le "Fram" n'atteignit pas le Pôle. La deuxième expédition (1898–1902) sous la direction d'Otto Sverdrup, explora le passage dit du Nord-Ouest, entre le Groënland et le Canada. La troisième expédition (1910–1914), conduite cette fois par Roald Amundsen, amena le "Fram" jusqu'à la barrière de glace, au Pôle Sud. Lui-même atteignit le Pôle le 14 Décembre 1911.
De ce fait, le "Fram" se trouve être le seul navire au monde à avoir poussé si loin, tant vers le Nord que vers le Sud.

El "Fram" esta ahora en puerto seguro en su propio edificio en Bygdøy. El buque fué construido para Fridtjof Nansen a fin de realizar su sueño que era dejarse llevar con hielo y corriente por el mar polar. En su primer viaje (1893–1896) el "Fram" navegó en el mar polar tal como estaba planeado, pero sin llegar al punto polar. En su segundo viaje (1898–1902) bajo la dirección de Otto Sverdrup, se exploró el pasaje llamado noreste entre Groenlandia y Canada y en su tercer viaje (1910–1914) "Fram" navegó bajo el mando de Roald Amundsen hasta la barrera de hielo del Polo Sur. Personalmente Amundsen alcanzó el punto polar el 14de diciembre de 1911. Por lo tanto el "Fram" es el buque del mundo que ha estado más al norte y más al sur.

Norsk Folkemuseum er landets største
friluftsmuseum med 170 bygninger hentet
fra forskjellige distrikter i landet. Bygningene
er rikt utstyrt med innbo fra de respektive
tidsperioder. Dessuten har museet store
samlinger som viser vår kulturelle utvikling
blant fattig og rik, i by og på land. Til høyere
ser vi Setesdaltunet.

With its 170 ancient buildings drawn from
different regions of Norway, the Norwegian
Folk Museum is the biggest open-air museum
in the country. The buildings are richly
provided with period furniture and household
utensils. Also on exhibition are comprehensive collections illustrating cultural
developments among rich and poor in town
and country. Right: Farm buildings from
Setesdal.

Das Norwegische Volksmuseum ist das
grösste Freilichtmuseum des Landes mit 170
Gebäuden, die man aus den verschiedenen
Bezirken im Lande nach Oslo transportierte.
Die Häuser sind reich mit Inventar der
respektiven Zeitepochen ausgestattet.
Ausserdem hat das Museum grosse Samm-
lungen, die unsere kulturelle Entwicklung
unter Arm und Reich, in Stadt und Land,
zeigen. Rechts sehen wir den Setesdal-
Hofplatz.

Le Musée Folklorique de Bygdøy est le plus
vaste Musée de plein air en Norvège. Ses 170
bâtiments proviennent des différentes régions
du pays et sont équipés de l'inventaire
corespondant à leur époque. En outre, de
riches collections permettent d'y suivre
l'évolution culturelle de la population – riche
ou pauvre, rurale ou urbaine. A droite, la
ferme de Setesdal.

El Museo Popular Nacional es el mayor
museo al aire libre del país, con 170 edificios
recuperados de distintos distritos del mismo.
Los edificios estan ricamente equipados con
articulos de las respectivas épocas. Además
el museo cuenta con grandes colecciones que
muestran nuestro desarrollo cultural tanto de
los humildes como de los ricos, centros
urbanos y campestres. A la derecha vemos
Setesdaltunet.

Gol stavkirke som opprinnelig var bygget (ca. 1200) på Gol i Hallingdal, er Norsk Folkemuseums største klenodium, vakkert plassert på det høyeste punkt i området.

Gol Stave Church. Originally built in about 1200 at Gol in the Hallingdal Valley, this church, the Norwegian Folk Museum's most prized possession, stands on the highest point in the grounds.

Die Gol Stabkirche, die ursprünglic in Gol im Hallingdal (ca. 1200) geba wurde, ist das grösste Kleinod des Norwegischen Volksmuseums, hübs placiert auf dem höchsten Punkt im Gebiet.

Joliment placée sur le point culminant du Musée, l'église en bois-debout, construite vers 1200 à Gol dans le Hallingdal, constitue le joya de l'ensemble.

La Iglesia de madera de Gol que originalmente fué construida en 120 en Gol de Hallingdal, es la joya má grande del Museo Popular Naciona preciosamente situada en el punto más alto del area.

Øverst ser vi et stabbur fra Hallingdal (til venstre) og interiør fra Bjørnebergstølstua, også fra Hallingdal. Nederst ser vi Numedalstunet (til venstre) og bur og loft fra Telemark.

Above: A storehouse ("stabbur") from the Hallingdal Valley and (top right) the interior of Bjørnebergstølstua, a house from the same valley. Left: Farm buildings from Numedal and (right) storehouses from Telemark.

Oben sehen wir einen "Stabbur" (Vorratsspeicher) aus Hallingdal (links) sowie Interieur von der "Björnebergstölstua", einem Häuschen ebenfalls aus Hallingdal. Ganz unten sehen wir den Hofplatz "Numedalstunet" (links) sowie Bauer und Speicher aus Telemark.

En haut, à gauche, une resserre de Hallingdal et l'intérieur du châlet d'alpage de Bjørneberg (Hallingdal). En bas, à gauche, la ferme de Numedal et deux petits bâtiments de ferme de Telemark.

Arriba vemos una casa de almacenamiento de comestibles de Hallingdal (a la izquierda) y el interior de la casita de Bjørneberg, también de Hallingdal. Abajo vemos el atrio de Numedal (a la izquierda) y casas de Telemark.

1. Edv. Munch: Selvportrett 1893, litografi.
2. Halfdan Egedius: Spill og dans 1896, olje.
3. Edv. Munch: Stemmen 1893, olje.

1. Edvard Munch: Self-portrait (1893). Lithograph.
2. Halfdan Egedius: Music and Dance (1896). Oil.
3. Edvard Munch: The Voice (1893). Oil.

1. Edv. Munch: Selbstporträt
   1893, Lithographie.
2. Halfdan Egedius: Spiel und
   Tanz 1896, Öl.
3. Edv. Munch: Die Stimme,
   1893, Öl.

1. Edv. Munch: Autoportrait
   1893, lithographie.
2. Halfdan Egedius: Violon et
   danse 1896, huile.
3. Edv. Munch: La Voix 1893,
   huile.

1. Edv. Munch: Autoretrato
   1893, óleo.
2. Halfdan Egedius: Música y
   baile 1893, óleo.
3. Edv. Munch: La voz 1893,
   óleo.

Oslo Universitet, Blindern
Oslo University, Blindern
Oslo Universität, Blindern
L'Université de Oslo, Blindern
La Universidad de Oslo,
Blindern

Fra de gamle industriområder
ved Akerselva

From the old industrial areas by
Akerselva

Anblick der alten Industrie
gelände an der Akerselva

Les anciennes industries qui
bordent Akerselva

Desde las antiquas zonas
industriales a orillas del rio
Aker

Oslo er berømt for sine vakre omgivelser, og her finner vi en av verdens mest berømte vinter-sportsarenaer, Holmenkollbakken. Verdens-mesterskapsarenaen 1982.

Oslo is renowned for the beauty of its setting. In the hills above the city stands the Holmenkollen Ski Jump and its adjoining arena, venue of the 1982 World Skiing Championships and a name to conjure with in winter sports circles the world over.

Oslo ist wegen seiner schönen Umgebung be-rühmt, hier finden wir auch die berühmteste Wintersportarena der Welt, die Holmenkollen-Schanze. Weltmeisterschaftsarena 1982.

Oslo est réputé pour la beauté de ses environs. Ici, le grand tremplin de Holmenkollen, l'arène sportive la plus célèbre du monde. Arène du Championnat Mondial 1982.

Oslo es famosa por la belleza de sus alrededores y aqui apreciamos el complejo de deporte invernal más famoso mundo, el trampolín de Holmen-kollen. Sede del Capeonato Mundial de 1982.

kisporten har lange tradisjoner i
Norge, og i umiddelbar tilknytning
il Holmenkollbakken finner vi et
noderne skimuseum som viser
kisportens utvikling i Norge
jennom århundrer.

Skiing enjoys long-standing
traditions in Norway. Adjacent to
the Holmenkollen Ski Jump there
is a modern museum tracing the
evolution of this national sport over
the centuries.

Der Skisport hat in Norwegen
lange Traditionen, und gewisser-
massen mit der Holmenkollen-
schanze verbunden ist dort ein
modernes Skimuseum, das die
Entwicklung des Skisports in
Norwegen Jahrhunderte hindurch
zeigt.

Le ski est le sport traditionnel e
Norvège. A côté du tremplin
d'Holmenkollen, le musée mode
de ski qui relate l'histoire et le
développement du ski en Norvè
à travers les siècles.

El deporte del esquí cuenta con largas tradiciones en Noruega y junto a los Saltos de Holmenkollen tenemos un museo moderno de esquí que relfeja el desarrollo del deporte del esquí en Noruega a través de los siglos.

Norge er vintersportens hjemland og Oslo er hovedstaden
med et eldorado for skisport av alle slag

La Norvége, pays originaire des sports d'hiver, avec sa
capitale Oslo, un véritable paradis pour le ski

Norway is the homeland of winter sports
Oslo, the capital, is an eldorado for all sort of skiing
activities

Noruega es la Patria de los deportes de invierno y Oslo, su
capital, es "El Dorado" para el deporte del esqui en todos
sus tipos

Norwergen ist die Heimat des Wintersportes, und Oslo ist
die Hauptstadt und ein Eldorado aller möglichen
Schisportaktivitäten

En idyll langs Akerselva

An idyllic spot on the banks of Akerselva

Idyll entlang der Akerselva

Une idylle le long de Akerselva

Idilico lugar a orillas del rio Aker

Fra Oslomarka, Ullevålseter

Ullevalseter - from the countryside near Oslo

Oslomarka, Ullevalseter

Ullevalseter au coeur de Oslomarka

Desde "Oslomarka" (bosques alrededor de Oslo) - Ulleyålseter